Bach

Other books in this series

BACH
Imogen Holst

HANDEL
Stanley Sadie

BARTÓK
Everett Helm

HAYDN
H. C. Robbins Landon

BEETHOVEN
Stanley Sadie

LISZT
Alan Walker

BRITTEN
Imogen Holst

MENDELSSOHN
Michael Hurd

BYRD
Imogen Holst

ROSSINI
James Harding

CHOPIN
Joan Chissell

VAUGHAN WILLIAMS
Michael Hurd

DELIUS
Eric Fenby

WAGNER
Elaine Padmore

ELGAR
Michael Hurd

HOLST
Imogen Holst

THE GREAT COMPOSERS

BACH

by

IMOGEN HOLST

FABER & FABER

3 Queen Square

London

First published in 1965
by Faber and Faber Limited
3 Queen Square London WC1
Reprinted 1966 and 1974
Printed in Great Britain by
Whitstable Litho, Straker Brothers Ltd

ISBN 0 571 06219 9

Contents

ACKNOWLEDGEMENTS   *page* 13

I. BACH'S HOME IN EISENACH   15

II. SCHOOLDAYS IN OHRDRUF AND LÜNEBURG   20

III. ORGANIST AT ARNSTADT   28

IV. A YEAR IN MÜHLHAUSEN   35

V. COURT MUSICIAN AT WEIMAR   40

VI. INSTRUMENTAL MUSIC AT CÖTHEN   49

VII. DIRECTOR OF MUSIC IN LEIPZIG   60

VIII. COMPOSING AND TEACHING   67

IX. THE LAST TWELVE YEARS   79

X. THE REDISCOVERY OF BACH'S MUSIC   86

INDEX   93

Illustrations

PLATES

I. St. Michael's Church, Lüneburg, from a painting   *facing page*
by Joachim Burmeister, *c.* 1705, in the Lüneburg Museum   48

II. Bach at Cöthen, from a portrait by Johann Jakob Ihle, *c.*
1720, in the Bach Museum at Eisenach   49

III. Bach's musical handwriting. Prelude in D sharp minor from
The Forty-eight Preludes and Fugues, Vol. II, in the British Museum   78

IV. Bach in the last year of his life, from a portrait by an unknown
artist, *c.* 1749, in the possession of Walther R. Volbach, Fort
Worth, Texas   79

LINE ILLUSTRATIONS

1. Eisenach in the middle of the seventeenth century   *page* 16
From Matthäus Merian's *Topographia, c.* 1650

2. A harpsichord player in the early eighteenth century   23
From Johann Christoph Weigel's *Musikalisches Theatrum*, 1730

3. Lüneburg, from *Topographia*   24

4. A French dancer at the time of Louis XIV   26

5. Arnstadt, from *Topographia*   32

6. Mühlhausen, from *Topographia*   36

9

Illustrations

7. Details of the construction of an eighteenth-century *page* 38
   organ, from Dom Bédos de Celles' *L'Art du Facteur d'Orgues*

8. Weimar, from *Topographia* 41

9. Cöthen, from *Topographia* 50

10. A viola da gamba player, from *Musikalisches Theatrum* 51

11. Plan of Leipzig, with St. Thomas's Church in the centre 61
    foreground, from *Topographia*

12. St. Thomas's Church and School in 1723, from the *Ordnung* 63
    der Schule zu St. Thomae in the Leipzig Museum

13. A bassoon player, from *Musikalisches Theatrum* 69

14. A flautist, from *Musikalisches Theatrum* 70

15. A performance of church music in the early eighteenth 76
    century, from Johann Gottfried Walther's *Musikalisches Lexikon*, dedicated to Duke Ernst August of Weimar, and published in Leipzig in 1732

16. Frederick the Great playing the flute with his orchestra, from 83
    an engraving by P. Haas

17. The theme of *The Musical Offering*, in Bach's writing 83

Music Examples

(The examples are by Bach, except for those with another composer's name)

1. Chorale: 'When we are in the greatest need'   *page* 17
   (*Wenn wir in höchsten Nöten sind*) Traditional tune

2. Chorale: 'O World, I now must leave thee'   18
   (*O Welt, ich muss dich lassen*) Traditional tune

3. From Sonata I in G minor for violin   19

4. From Partita I in B minor for violin   19

5. Carol: *Es ist ein Ros entsprungen*, harmonized by Praetorius   21

6. From an Allemande from the *Suite ex gis* by Pachelbel   22

7. From a Rondeau by Couperin   26

8. Ornaments from the *Clavier-Büchlein*   27

9, 9a, 9b.   Chorale Variations: 'O God, thou gracious God'   29
   (*O Gott, du frommer Gott*)

10. From a Prelude by Buxtehude   33

11. From Cantata 161, 'Come, thou lovely hour of dying'   42
    (*Komm, du süsse Todesstunde*)

12, 12a.   Canon for his friend, J. G. Walther   44

13. Chorale Prelude: 'Christ, thou Lamb of God'   47
    (*Christe, du Lamm Gottes*)

Music Examples

14. Rondeau from the Suite in B minor for flute and orchestra *page* 52

15. Trio from the 1st Brandenburg Concerto   52

16. From Sonata II in A minor for violin   54

17. From Suite III in C major for cello   54

18. Prelude from the *Clavier-Büchlein*   56

19. *Gib dich zufrieden und sei stille*, from the 'Note-book for Anna Magdalena'   58

20. Extended Chorale from Cantata 140: 'Sleepers Wake!'   72
    (*Wachet auf*)

21. From the Pastoral Symphony in the *Christmas Oratorio*   75

22. Canonic Variation for organ: 'From heav'n on high I come to earth' (*Vom Himmel hoch da komm' ich her*)   81

23. Last chorus from the *St. Matthew Passion*   90

Acknowledgements

I wish to express my thanks to the following, who have kindly allowed me to reproduce copyright material: to Bärenreiter-Verlag, Kassel and Basel, for Plates II and IV from Heinrich Besseler, *Fünf echte Bildnisse Johann Sebastian Bachs*, for Figs. 1, 3, 5, 6, 8, 9 and 11 from *Johann Sebastian Bach, Documenta*, and for Figs. 2, 10, 13 and 14 from Johann Christoph Weigel, *Musikalisches Theatrum*; to the Museumsverein für das Fürstentum Lüneburg for Plate I; to the Museum der Bildenden Künste, Leipzig, for Fig. 12; to the Institut für Dokumentation, Deutsche Akademie der Wissenschaften in Berlin for Fig. 16; to the Trustees of the British Museum for Plate III, and Figs. 7, 15 and 17; to Miss Armide Oppé for Fig. 4; and to the Oxford University Press for permission to quote the translation of Bach's letter to Frederick the Great on page 83 from Charles Sanford Terry's *Bach. A Biography*, an enthralling book that is brimful of information. (Other letters and documents have been taken from the original German in Spitta's *Johann Sebastian Bach*, published in 1873, and from Forkel's biography, translated by a 'Mr. Stephenson' in 1808.)

I am also grateful to McWhirter Twins Ltd., *Facts and Figures for Publishers*, for giving me the approximate eighteenth-century English equivalents of the sums of money mentioned in the following chapters, and for the additional information that 'in the much more difficult question of today's values compared with those of say 1730, the factor varies widely for common goods and luxuries of that day: for many categories of goods (for example, a loaf of bread), a factor of $\times 50$ would not be too much'.

I

Bach's Home in Eisenach

When Johann Sebastian Bach was born in the German town of Eisenach on 21st March 1685, his parents had good reason to hope that he would become a musician when he grew up. For his family had been musicians for generations, and his three brothers already showed signs of following the example of their father and grandfather and great-grandfather.

In the towns and villages near Eisenach, throughout the whole district of Thuringia, there were uncles and great-uncles and first cousins and second cousins who earned their living as composers, singers, choir-masters, organists, violinists or trumpeters. These hard-working musicians were too busy to see very much of each other, but they managed to meet once a year at a 'family-day' in Eisenach or Arnstadt or some other Thuringian town, where they would make music together all day long. The family was so well known that people in Thuringia spoke of a 'Bach' or a 'musician' as if the two words meant the same thing.

Many years later, when Bach had children of his own, he wrote a short family history called *The Origin of the Musical Bachs*. It begins with a description of his great-great-grandfather: 'Veit Bach, a baker living in Hungary during the sixteenth century, was compelled to leave the country because he belonged to the Lutheran church. He went to Germany, and when he found that Lutherans were welcomed in Thu-

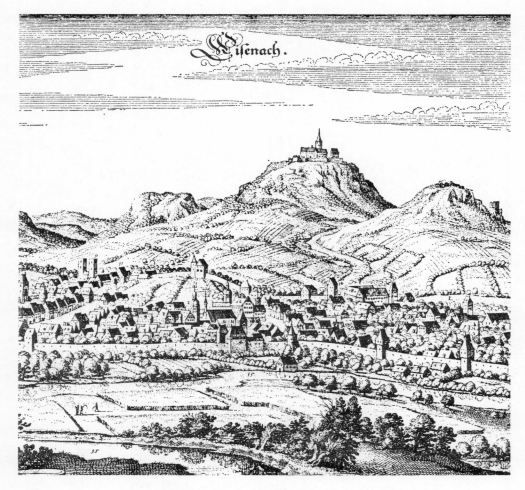

FIG. 1. *Eisenach in the middle of the seventeenth century*

ringia, he settled there and went on with his trade. He enjoyed practising
the cittern [an instrument like a small guitar], and he used to take
it with him into the mill whenever it was grinding. What a strange
sound the pair of them must have made together! However, it taught
him to keep time, and that is perhaps how music first came into our
family.'

Bach's father, Johann Ambrosius, was a professional violinist. His

16

fellow-townsmen in Eisenach spoke of him as 'a man of understanding and skill, respected by the whole community'. He was employed as a court musician to the Duke of Eisenach and had to play for the entertainment of any guests who were staying at the castle. He was also a member of the Town Musicians and had to play for local weddings and for occasional banquets in the Town Hall.

His home was an old two-storied house with a red-tiled attic roof; it had a huge open fire-place in the kitchen and a solid oak stair-case leading to a wide landing. From the windows there was a distant view of the ancient castle of the Wartburg, high up on the top of the hill. (See Fig. 1.) This was the castle where Martin Luther had been imprisoned for his own protection during the year 1521–22: he had spent his time there in beginning his translation of the Bible into German for the new church he was founding.

Eisenach had soon become a stronghold of the Lutheran faith, and from Sebastian Bach's earliest childhood he would have been told of Luther's love of music, and of his impatience with those 'over-religious' people who didn't approve of having it in church. He may also have been told of the legend of how Luther used to walk up and down playing folk-tunes on his flageolet while trying to fit their familiar rhythms to the words of the new hymns he had just written. Many of the Protestant tunes we now sing in church on Sundays were originally sung in the streets and the fields to words that had nothing to do with religion.

Ex.1 'When we are in the greatest need'

Ex.2 'O World, I now must leave thee'

The hymn tune 'When we are in the greatest need' (Ex. 1) began as a French folk song, and 'O World, I now must leave thee' (Ex. 2) was once a well-known German love song.

Sebastian would have heard these tunes when he was still in his cradle, for his family were devout members of the Lutheran church. And when he was eight he must have felt proud to be going to the school where Luther had been a pupil two hundred years before him. Here he learnt the Catechism, the Psalms and Bible history. He also learnt elementary Latin grammar from an interesting text-book of 'useful facts' which had cheerful pictures on every page.

On Sundays he sang with the members of the school choir in St. George's Church, where his father's cousin, Christoph Bach, was organist. There were probably many occasions when he was allowed to sit in the organ loft and pull out the stops while Christoph was practising.

Living in a musician's house, with brothers who were learning to play instruments, Sebastian would have felt as much at home in the language of music as in the language of words. By the time he was going to school his father had begun giving him violin lessons. Although we do not know what pieces he learnt we can guess that he would have practised scales and broken chords in the lively style of the late seven-

Ex.3 Presto

etc.

Ex.4 Presto

etc.

teenth century, prolonging some of the notes and repeating others until the exercises turned themselves into the sort of tunes he himself was to write many years later. (See Exs. 3 and 4.)

But the exciting violin lessons came to an abrupt end, for his parents died within a year of each other. His eldest brother, Johann Christoph, offered to adopt him, and on a wintry February day, a few weeks before his tenth birthday, he said goodbye to his home in Eisenach and set out with his brothers on the thirty mile journey to Ohrdruf.

19

II

Schooldays in Ohrdruf and Lüneburg

The new home in Ohrdruf was a small cottage near St. Michael's Church, where Johann Christoph was organist. Sebastian's thirteen-year-old brother Johann Jakob had come with him to keep him company, and they were looked after by Johann Christoph's newly-married wife. In the next street was the school where they went for lessons in religion, reading, writing, arithmetic, singing and elementary natural science.

This school had recently become famous for its experimental methods of teaching: the children were encouraged to 'learn by doing', and the results were so successful that the agricultural workers from the villages near Ohrdruf were better educated than many of the noblemen's sons who were living in other districts.

Sebastian started learning Greek when he was ten, in a class where the average age was twelve. He was soon top of his class, and before his thirteenth birthday he began studying theology. He must have found the subject enthralling, for when he grew up he had as many as eighty books about theology on his shelves.

Meanwhile he was learning a great deal about music from his brother Johann Christoph. In his harmony lessons he learnt the difference between consonant and dissonant intervals; he learnt that every note has its 'own' chord consisting of the note itself and the third and the fifth above it; and he also learnt that figures such as $\frac{6}{2}$ or $\frac{6}{3}$ or $\frac{7}{3}$ represented those particular

Schooldays in Ohrdruf and Lüneburg

Ex.5 CAROL   Harmonised by Praetorius

intervals above a given bass note. He could recognize cadences by exploring a familiar hymn such as Ex. 5, where 'the natural flow of the music' taught him that 'each voice must have an individual tune of its own', and that 'all the voices must combine agreeably'.

Johann Christoph also gave him lessons on the organ, the harpsichord and the clavichord. In his technical studies he may possibly have taught him the new method of holding his hands over the keys with the fingers curved instead of straight, so that the thumbs could be used. (Years afterwards, this was the method Bach taught his own pupils, when he himself was a teacher.)

Sebastian's progress was astonishing: we are told that 'no sooner had his brother given him a piece to play than he demanded another, more difficult'. There is a story, often quoted by biographers, which says that Johann Christoph possessed a volume of pieces by some of the most celebrated living composers such as Buxtehude, Böhm and Pachelbel, and that Sebastian had begged, unsuccessfully, to be allowed to borrow it. It was kept locked up in a cupboard, but the door had a latticed panel and Sebastian managed to get his small hands through the crevices, and after several attempts he succeeded in dragging out the paper-bound volume. He decided to copy it in secret. He was not allowed a candle in his bedroom, so he had to wait for moonlit nights before he could write out the pieces. At the end of six months he had finished the last piece, but in an unlucky moment his brother discovered the newly-written copy and took it away from him.

This story might seem to suggest that Johann Christoph was a very unsympathetic brother, but it is more likely that he was nothing worse than a very conscientious teacher, who believed that the startlingly unfamiliar keys in Ex. 6 were too bewildering for any twelve-year-old pupil.

He could not have realized that the future composer of *The Forty-eight Preludes and Fugues* was already able to take double flats in his stride.

Sebastian spent five years in his brother's home, reaching the top class in the Ohrdruf school. By that time Johann Christoph was finding it difficult to make room for him in the cottage, as he now had three small children of his own. Fortunately one of the music masters at the school solved the problem by arranging that Sebastian and one of his school friends should be entered as choral scholars at the choir school of St. Michael's, Lüneburg, which was the equivalent of our present-day choir school at King's College, Cambridge. Therefore in March 1700,

FIG. 2. *A harpsichord player in the early eighteenth century*

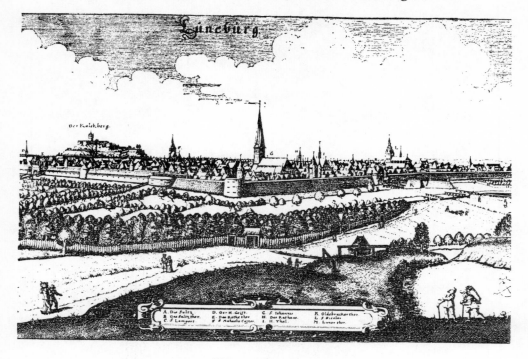

FIG. 3. *Lüneburg*

a few days before his fifteenth birthday, he left with his school-friend Erdmann for the distant city in the north of Germany.

His first glimpse of St. Michael's must have been unforgettable. He had never seen a church with such lofty pillars or such spacious aisles. (See Plate 1.) The acoustics were superb, and the sound of the music for Easter Sunday was a revelation, with its choir of trained singers and its instrumental accompaniment of strings, flutes, oboes, bassoons, horns, trumpets, trombones and timpani. Those in charge of the music welcomed Sebastian, as he was a reliable sight-reader with a clear soprano voice. Although his voice broke when he had been there only a few months, he was able to prove himself equally reliable as a violinist. And it is more than likely that the school authorities made use of him as a copyist.

The library at St. Michael's had a remarkably large collection of church music of the sixteenth and seventeenth centuries. There were

24

masses and motets by Italian and Flemish composers, written in the earlier, polyphonic style of Palestrina. And there were the new 'sacred concerts', or cantatas, with dramatic dialogues and instrumental interludes, written by living German composers who had been influenced by the recent invention of opera. It was a wonderful opportunity for Sebastian to be able to study the scores of these contemporary works and to hear them performed during the Sunday services.

Sometimes he was able to meet the composers and talk to them. J. J. Löwe, whose music was often sung at St. Michael's, was organist at the nearby church of St. Nicholas, and he made friends with Sebastian and told him about his old teacher, the great Heinrich Schütz, who had been the first composer to bring the splendours of Venetian music into Germany. Then there was Georg Böhm, organist of St. John's Church in Lüneburg. He was one of the 'celebrated composers' of the forbidden volume in far-off Ohrdruf, and now, only three years later, he was giving Sebastian helpful advice about his own organ compositions. Böhm had been a pupil of the famous organist Reinken of Hamburg, and his description of his teacher's playing made such an impression on Sebastian that he decided to walk to Hamburg during the summer holidays and try and hear the old man, who was now in his eightieth year.

The journey to Hamburg was long and tiring, but it was well worth it, for when he reached St. Catherine's Church he heard Reinken improvising on the magnificent organ for over half an hour on end. On the return journey, when he was feeling particularly tired and hungry, he sat down to rest outside an inn and wished he could have afforded to have gone inside for a meal. Suddenly someone threw two herring's heads out of the kitchen window, straight into his lap. And when he picked them up he found a Danish ducat (worth £1 1s.) inside each head. (The story sounds like a legend, but Bach himself many years later used to enjoy hearing it repeated by his own children.)

Another journey that he made at about this time was to Celle, where the Duke of Lüneburg had built a beautifully designed small theatre for the performance of the latest operas and ballets. There is no record of

FIG. 4. *A French dancer at the time of Louis XIV*

Ex.7 RONDEAU   Couperin

smooth and graceful

Ex.8

how Sebastian managed to get inside the theatre, but it was probably as a deputy violinist in the orchestra. Here, for the first time, he saw French dancing and followed the intricate movements of the slow Sarabande, the stately Minuet, the cheerful Bourée and the lively Gigue. (See Fig. 4.) And here he heard French harpsichord pieces, including the Rondeau in Ex. 7, which he liked so much that he copied it out for his own use on future occasions.

He also copied out some of the French 'grace-notes', those expressive ornaments that he was already using in his instrumental music. (See Ex. 8.)

If he had wanted to, he could probably have stayed on in Celle, earning his living in the orchestra. But church music came first in his life, and now that he was nearly eighteen he felt that the time had come when he should apply for an organist's post in his own native Thuringia.

III

Organist at Arnstadt

It was in Arnstadt that Bach began earning a regular living. The town had been employing members of his family for nearly a century, so the councillors were quite ready to listen to the eighteen-year-old student trying out the organ that had just been built for the New Church. And when they heard his playing they thought so highly of him that they decided to appoint him as organist, in spite of his youth and his lack of professional experience.

The conditions of his work were clearly set out in his contract; 'Whereas our Noble and Gracious Count of Schwarzburg-Arnstadt has been pleased to appoint you, Johann Sebastian Bach, as organist of the New Church, now therefore you shall be faithful, loyal and obedient to his Lordship, proving yourself industrious in your calling, taking no part in other affairs or occupations; attending on Sundays and other Festivals at the organ entrusted to you, and playing thereon as is required of you. You shall be diligent in reporting if any part thereof should fall into disrepair, and at all times shall be heedful that it be kept in good order. In your daily conduct you shall be God-fearing, sober and well-disposed to all men, proving yourself an honourable servant before God and your Worshipful Masters. For this you shall receive for yearly pay 50 florins (£6 5s.) and for board and lodging 30 thalers (£7 10s). Given under the signature and seal of his Lordship's Chancellery this day, August 9th, 1703.' (See end of page 13 for a note on eighteenth-century money.)

Organist at Arnstadt

Bach found lodgings at the Golden Crown Inn. The landlord had been one of the first parishioners to help raise money for building the new organ, so he must have enjoyed talking to his young lodger about it and hearing him describe each of the twenty-eight stops in detail.

Bach had never before had an organ entirely for his own use, and one can imagine how he rejoiced at the chance of working for long hours every day. The organ pieces he wrote at this time were mostly Chorale Preludes, described as 'preambling to the Chorale', and Chorale Variations, such as Exs. 9a and 9b, where he varied the rhythm and texture of the hymn in Ex. 9 without destroying its clear outline, so that members of the congregation could recognize the tune.

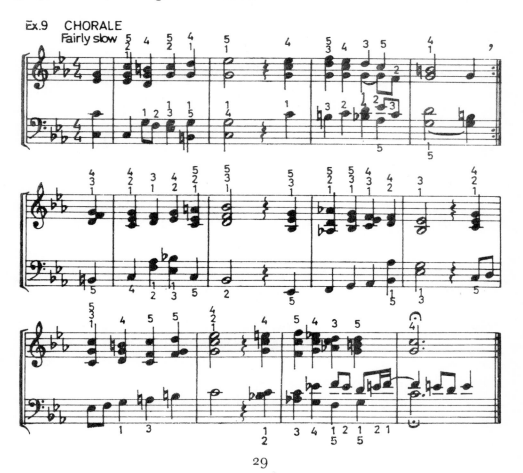

Ex.9a VARIATION

(Bach very rarely gave any hints about what fingering to use. The fingering in this book has been added for the sake of readers who want to play the keyboard examples on the piano. The organ pieces are much easier if they are treated as duets, with one stave of the music to each player. Avoid overpedalling, as it smudges the tunes. Notes that move step-wise are usually smooth: leaps of a fifth or an octave are often staccato.)

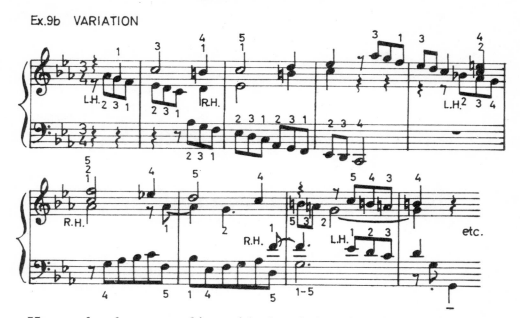

Ex.9b VARIATION

He was less happy working with the choir. The task of training the singers should really have been undertaken by a 'Cantor' or Director of Music, but the church authorities expected Bach to combine this with the post of organist although it had not been mentioned in his contract. The choir-boys had got into bad habits, and the Council complained that even in school hours they showed no respect for their masters but fought in front of them and played games in the class-rooms, while out of school they had been seen drinking and gambling in the beer-houses, and had frequently disturbed elderly householders by their unruly shouting late at night. As Bach was only a few months older than his own choir-boys he found it difficult to keep order, and he often lost his temper with them.

He also lost his temper with some of the older students. There was a bassoon-player whose high notes sounded to Bach's ears exactly like the bleating of a nanny-goat. Unfortunately he was tactless enough to mention this to his friends, who immediately passed it round among the other students. The bassoon player was furious. The next time he met Bach in the street he threatened him with a stick: Bach quickly drew his

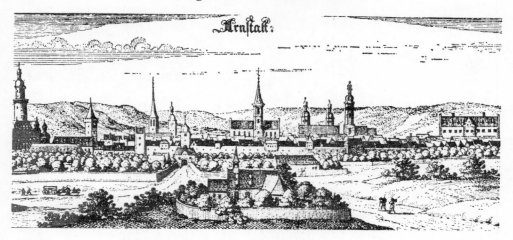

FIG. 5. *Arnstadt*

sword, and the 'nanny-goat's' companions had to separate them. This undignified skirmish was reported to the authorities. Bach was summoned to their presence and told that he must learn to get on better with people who were not such good musicians as he was himself.

Soon after this he asked for four weeks leave of absence, so that he might go to Lübeck, in the north of Germany, to hear the great organist-composer Dietrich Buxtehude. Permission was granted, and he arranged that his cousin Johann Ernst Bach should deputize for him while he was away.

There is a tradition that he walked the whole distance of three hundred miles, but it is more likely that he was given several lifts on the way. He reached Lübeck in October, just in time to hear the famous *Evening Music* in St. Mary's church, conducted by Buxtehude. It was astonishingly dramatic music, with passionate dialogues between singers representing Good and Evil, and with thrilling instrumental contrasts between Heaven and Hell. Bach had never heard music on such a scale as this: there were forty players in the orchestra. Nor had he seen such vast audiences: on two occasions the authorities had to have twenty soldiers on guard at the church doors to control the crowds that were trying to fight their way in.

Lübeck was also famous for its organ music, and for hour after hour

Organist at Arnstadt

Bach was able to listen to Buxtehude playing Preludes and Fugues or Toccatas and Fantasias. He was enthralled by the composer's vitality and invention: the simplest scales and arpeggios were transformed into brilliant cascades and glittering ripples of sound, as in Ex. 10.

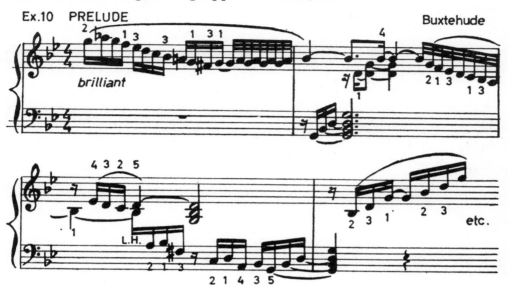

Buxtehude was growing old, and he was looking for a successor. Bach could have added fresh glories to the music-making in the church, and he might have accepted the post and spent the rest of his life in Lübeck if it had not been for an extraordinary clause in the contract which stated that the new organist had got to marry Buxtehude's daughter. She was then thirty, and as Bach was only twenty he felt it was too heavy a price to pay for the privilege of having such good singers and players to work with. He stayed as long as he dared, and then reluctantly said goodbye to the greatest composer he was ever to meet.

By the time he got back to Arnstadt he had been away nearly four months instead of four weeks, and he found that he was in disgrace with the authorities. No sooner had he begun work again than there were complaints about his organ playing. His improvisations, inspired by Buxtehude, were too elaborate and 'audacious' for the congregation. And they went on far too long: the services were held up by such exuberant outpourings of sound. Bach's reply to this criticism was characteristic: he went to the other extreme and made his introductions so short that he reached the hymn before anyone was ready for it.

Then there was another cause for complaint. Members of the Council had heard a young girl singing in the organ gallery while Bach was playing in the empty church. This was his cousin Maria Barbara Bach, whom he hoped to marry. As it happened he had asked the Pastor's permission for her to be in the church while he practised, and the Council's interference made him so angry that he decided to look for another post where he would have more freedom and better working conditions. His organ playing was already being spoken of in other towns in Thuringia, and when one of the organists at Mühlhausen died Bach was offered the post and accepted it.

IV

A Year in Mühlhausen

When he arrived in Mühlhausen in the summer of 1707 Bach found the city in a state of utter confusion. A fortnight earlier there had been a disastrous fire which had destroyed four hundred houses: the flames had reached to within a few yards of the ancient church of St. Blaise where he was to be organist. Several of the councillors had lost all their possessions: they had to borrow pen and ink before they could sign their names to the document appointing him to his new post.

In the list of conditions set out in this document Bach promised 'to have at heart the welfare of the Free Imperial City of Mühlhausen, and to contribute thereto'. His yearly salary was to be eighty-five gulden, (£10 12s. 6d.) with an allowance of three measures of corn, two trusses of wood, and six trusses of faggots delivered to his door. And the councillors agreed to send a wagon to Arnstadt to fetch his belongings to his new home in the suburb beyond the medieval walls of the city.

This small house was to become his home in a very real sense of the word. For owing to a legacy of fifty gulden (£6 5s.) from his mother's brother he was able to marry his cousin Maria Barbara. The wedding took place in October in the village church at Dornheim: the bride and bridegroom had known the young Pastor there when he had been a theological student in Arnstadt. During their six-day honeymoon they visited as many of their relations as possible, and we must hope that they

Fig. 6. *Mühlhausen*

were given some presents of knives and forks and pots and pans, for until then Bach's only possessions had been his books and music and instruments.

At Mühlhausen one of his earliest tasks was to write a cantata for the annual inauguration service of the City Councillors. There were forty-eight of them, and they took it in turn to manage the city's affairs, sixteen at a time, for one year. The Archdeacon of Mühlhausen provided a libretto, founded on Psalm 47, which Bach set in a splendour of trumpets and drums, basing his music on the hymn tune in Ex. 9.

This cantata, *God is my King*, is one of the most magnificent he ever wrote. His employers may have mistakenly supposed that one or two of its fanfares were being composed in their honour, but in Bach's mind there was no doubt at all that every bar of the music was written to the glory of God. (He always headed his manuscripts with the words 'Jesu, help': and when he had reached the last double bar he added the initials 'S.D.G.' for 'Soli Deo Gloria'.)

The councillors took the preparations for the ceremony so seriously that they actually allowed money to be spent on publishing *God is my King*: it is the only one of all the cantatas Bach wrote that he ever saw in print.

The church of St. Blaise was too small for the huge congregation, so the performance took place in the larger church of St. Mary's. The organist had the responsibility of playing the 'continuo' accompaniment to the choruses from Bach's figured bass part, in which only the bass notes were written out with numbers underneath them to show what chords were to be played. (See page 20, last line.) The actual bass notes were strengthened by the addition of a bassoon and a 'violone', the seventeenth and early eighteenth-century version of our double bass.

There is no organ part given for the solos in *God is my King*, so it is possible that Bach accompanied them himself on the harpsichord.

The texture of figured bass accompaniment was very much in Bach's mind at this time. He mentioned it in his report on the condition of the organ at St. Blaise's, informing the Council that 'the 8ft trumpet stop on the upper manual must be replaced by a 16 ft. "fagotto" [i.e. a double bassoon] which will introduce a new blending of the tone and will allow for a more delicate accompaniment in figured bass.' There were other improvements that he suggested: the pressure of wind-power was to be increased, so that the lowest notes of the pedals would be audible; this would also help in avoiding unsteadiness of tone. It is interesting to see that he insisted that 'the tremulant should be made to vibrate properly.' Many people think of the tremulant stop as a sentimental sound belonging to the weakest sort of nineteenth-century music. But it was far from sentimental in Bach's hands. He used it as a colour, as part of the richly ornamental style of early eighteenth-century music; a style that is sometimes called 'Baroque', because it is the equivalent of Baroque architecture, with its twisted pillars and elaborate scroll-work.

In making his suggestions for improving the Mühlhausen organ Bach never forgot the practical side of the craft of organ-building. He mentioned the actual materials the new pipes should be made of; one of them should be wood instead of metal, as it would be more resonant; another, with an oboe tone, should be made of good quality tin, '14 parts pure to 2 parts alloy'.

The church authorities saw that he knew what he was talking about and they agreed to all his suggestions. But Bach had left the Free Imperial City before the work on the organ had been finished. He made up his mind not to stay any longer when he found that the Pastor of St. Blaise's had been influenced by a revivalist preacher who wanted to get rid of

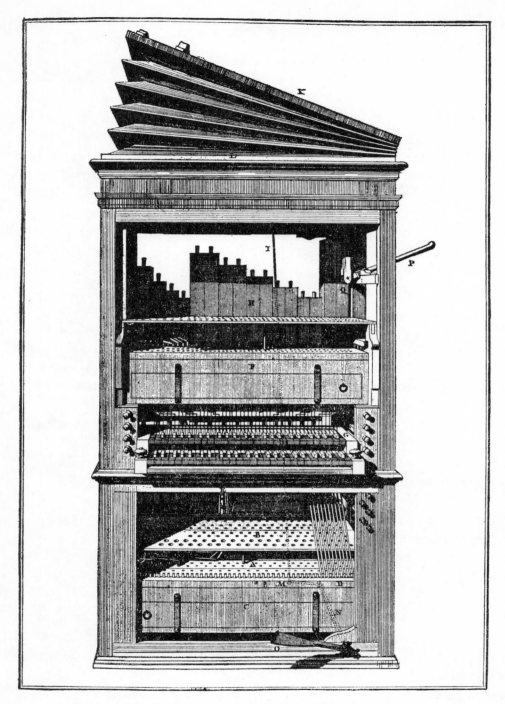

FIG. 7. *Details of the construction of an eighteenth century organ*

music in the church service. In Bach's letter of resignation, addressed to 'the Honourable and Distinguished Parochial Councillors', he wrote: ' . . . It has always been my aim to carry out your wishes that church music should be performed to the glory of God, and as far as I have been able I have also worked towards this end in the surrounding villages, where a love of music is growing, and where the singing and playing is often better than in our own city churches . . . At all times I have cheerfully fulfilled my tasks, but I have not been able to do my work without opposition. Also, if I may say so without disrespect, although my household economy has been frugal, I have not had enough to live on. God has been pleased, however, to open the door to a new situation in the service of His Serene Highness the Duke of Sachsen-Weimar. This offers a more adequate salary, and the opportunity to strive towards the goal that most concerns me, that is, the betterment of church music . . . I therefore humbly beg your generous permission to retire.'

This letter, in spite of its formal language, tells us a good deal about Bach as a person. The reference to village churches proves that although he could lose his temper with the 'nanny-goat' type of player he could be patient with a genuine learner and, like other great composers in other centuries, could draw surprisingly good music from a small gathering of amateurs.

The letter also shows his characteristic determination to stand up for his rights. And it shows that he already knew, at the age of twenty-three, that his life was to be concerned with 'the betterment of church music'.

The councillors who employed him had to accept his resignation. 'Since he has made up his mind,' they said, 'we shall have to let him go.' But there was no ill-feeling on either side, and when the improvements to the St. Blaise organ were finished Bach revisited Mühlhausen and played a Chorale Prelude on the hymn-tune 'A Stronghold Sure', using the new bassoon stop he had asked for.

Meanwhile, in the summer of 1708, he and his wife packed up their belongings after less than a year in their first home, and set out for Weimar.

V

Court Musician at Weimar

Bach's new employer, Duke Wilhelm Ernst of Weimar, was a man of exceedingly serious disposition. At the age of seven he had preached a sermon on faith and duty to a large congregation of respectful courtiers. Since then he had spent much of his time in good works, founding a home for orphans and a training centre for theological students. Life in the castle was austere: there was a strict rule that lights should be out at 8 p.m. in winter and 9 p.m. in summer.

The Duke was chiefly interested in the services that were held in the royal chapel. In spite of his severity he believed that music was a necessary part of those services, and he employed a small orchestra to accompany the choir in a cantata every Sunday. The players, Bach among them, were dressed in the uniform of Hungarian hussars: a tall cloth cap, a jacket trimmed with braid, tight breeches, high boots, and a short cloak hanging from the left shoulder. The chapel where they played was a cold, unfriendly building dating from the mid-seventeenth century. The walls and ceiling were pale mauve, and three ornately arched storeys rose from a reddish-brown tiled floor. The second storey had jade-green pillars, while projecting from the third storey, and mounted on grey stone plinths, were twenty enormous classical busts: judging from the only surviving picture of the chapel, they must have been of a repellent ugliness. High above these statues, just under the roof, was the musicians' gallery with an organ that was not as good as the one Bach had had in Mühlhausen.

Fig. 8. *Weimar*

The gallery was small, and there was so little space for the orchestra that the violinists can scarcely have found enough room to draw their bows across the strings at the climax of a crescendo. This must have been a real cause of distress to Bach, as he was always very particular about placing his instrumentalists where their playing would sound best. To add to the discomfort, the chapel was icy cold. The players, when left to themselves, preferred to rehearse in their own lodgings, but before long a notice was put up saying that 'it was expressly ordered that rehearsals should always take place in the chapel', and Bach's salary had to be supplemented with an allowance for firewood and charcoal for the organ gallery, 'to tide him through the winter'.

It was here that he spent nine years of his life. In 1714 he was appointed 'Conzertmeister', which meant that he was second in command to the

41

Ex.11 'Come, thou lovely hour of dying'

etc.

chief musician, or 'Capellmeister', an old man who had been in the Duke's service for a long time. Bach's duties included composing a new cantata every month: an entry in the castle account books mentions '12 reams of paper to Conzertmeister Bach for the cantatas in the chapel'.

Fortunately he found just the right man to provide his texts for him. The Duke's librarian, Salomo Franck, was a sensitive poet and a passionately sincere Christian. The two men worked together in close friendship, and Bach, whose music was always guided by the meaning of the text, wrote some of his loveliest tunes as a result of their collaboration. The well-known *Jesu, Joy of Man's Desiring* belongs to these years in Weimar. And the simple, flowing tune for recorders in *Come, Thou Lovely Hour of Dying* shows that Bach's tranquil attitude to death was shared by the poet he was working with. (See Ex. 11.)

Other friends in Weimar included the Duke's young nephews, Prince Ernst August, and Prince Johann Ernst, who both had lessons from Bach. Johann Ernst was a gifted player and a promising composer: he had made a special study of Italian instrumental music, and it was possibly he who introduced the music of Vivaldi to Bach. (We are told by Bach's first biographer, Forkel, that Vivaldi's concertos for violin and orchestra served Bach as 'a kind of guide: he so often heard them praised as admirable compositions that he conceived the happy idea of arranging them for the keyboard'.)

The young organist of the town church in Weimar, Johann Gottfried Walther, was already a friend, for he was related to Bach's mother. The two musicians used to send each other ingenious little canons in their spare time, in the same casual fashion in which a couple of university dons might exchange Greek limericks on a winter's evening. (See Ex. 12 and the beginning of the 'working-out' in Ex. 12a. The use of the C clef in Ex. 12, showing the line for 'middle' C, makes it possible for the canon to be read from the same stave at the four different levels of pitch. If Ex. 12a is written out in full it can be played on four recorders; descant, treble, tenor and bass, with the treble playing an octave higher. After the repeat, the four instruments go back to the beginning, ending with a pause on the last note shown in Ex. 12a.)

Ex.12 CANON

At a moderate speed

Ex.12a

etc.

Court Musician at Weimar

Bach and Walther often made music together, and there is a story about them which shows how well they knew each other. Bach had been telling Walther that he was able to sight-read any music that was put in front of him. Walther said nothing, but thought of a trick that he could play on him. The next time Bach called on his friend there was no one to welcome him, but seeing an unfamiliar piece of music propped up on the harpsichord he sat down and began to play it. Very soon he reached a bar where the notes defeated him. He went back to the beginning, but broke down again in just the same place. At that moment there was a cheerful laugh from the next room and Walther came in, delighted at the success of his plot.

This story is one of the many anecdotes that found their way into the earliest of Bach's biographies. Not all of them are to be believed, but it seems likely that this particular anecdote is true, for it is typical of Bach that he should choose to repeat a story against himself. Like other really great artists, he had a clear idea of what he could achieve, and he was utterly incapable of being pompous or of showing off. On one occasion, when an admirer had complimented him on his wonderful organ playing, he said 'There's nothing wonderful about it; you just put down the right notes and the organ does the rest!'

Owing to his fame as an organist he was often invited to city churches to inspect their new organs and to report on them. As always, he was scrupulously accurate in his criticism and thoroughly practical in his advice. At Halle he told them that the bellows had been placed too near the west window: a curtain should be hung there in summer to protect the instrument from the hot sunshine. He also told them that the organ-builder was not to be blamed because the gilded pipes were dull instead of shining: they had become coated with soot from the grimy atmosphere.

We do not know what music Bach played on this Halle organ during the service of dedication, but we know what he had to eat at the banquet after the service, for a copy of the menu has survived. It mentions '*boeuf à la mode*; pike with anchovy sauce; smoked ham; dish of peas; dish of potatoes; sausages; quarter of roast mutton; boiled pumpkin; fritters; candied lemon peel; preserved cherries; asparagus; lettuce; radishes.'

45

There was also a formal visit to Cassel, when he was in attendance on the Duke of Weimar. On this occasion an Hereditary Prince, who was afterwards to become King of Sweden, was so astounded by Bach's organ playing that he pulled the ring off his finger and gave it to him: a mark of appreciation that greatly impressed the courtiers who were standing by. One of the listeners described the scene long afterwards, saying that Bach's feet 'went flying over the pedals as though they were winged, making the notes reverberate like thunder in a storm.'

In Dresden a public organ contest was arranged between Bach and Marchand, a celebrated French organist who had been one of the court musicians at Versailles. There are confusing and contradictory accounts of what happened, but it seems that the Frenchman disappeared from Dresden on the morning of the contest, leaving Bach to give a solo recital to an enraptured audience who proclaimed him 'the prince of organists'.

But in the castle at Weimar things were not going so well. The old Capellmeister had died, and Bach naturally expected the Duke to promote him to the position of authority. But the old man's son was made Capellmeister, and Bach was bitterly disappointed.

There were other causes for misgiving. Life at court was becoming more and more uncomfortable owing to the Duke's frequent quarrels with his nephew Ernst August. Members of the Duke's orchestra were forbidden to visit the nephew, and anyone who was seen talking to him was to be fined ten thalers (£2 10s.). This was more than Bach was prepared to put up with, and when Prince Leopold of Anhalt-Cöthen offered him the post of Capellmeister at his court, he decided that the time had come to leave Weimar, and he sent in his resignation. The Duke refused to release him. Bach wrote a second letter, obstinately insisting that he should be allowed to choose whom he worked for. The Duke replied by having him put under arrest.

The month that Bach spent in the Justice Room at the castle was not wasted, for he quietly went on with his own work, making the most of the long days of enforced solitude. He was writing his *Little Organ Book*, in which 'a Beginner at the Organ is given Instruction in treating a Chorale in different ways, at the same time gaining Facility in the Use of the Ped-

Flowing

als'. (Ex. 13 shows one of the many ways in which he treats the hymn tune in canon over a flowing counter-subject: it is easy to play on the piano if three players each take a single stave of the music.)

Bach worked at these organ pieces throughout the month of November 1717. At the beginning of December the Duke grudgingly released him, and he was able to leave Weimar for Cöthen.

PLATE I. *St. Michael's Church, Lüneburg*

PLATE II. *Bach at Cöthen*

VI

Instrumental Music at Cöthen

The first few years that Bach spent in Cöthen were probably the happiest of his whole working life. His new employer, the young Prince Leopold, was, in Bach's own words, 'a gracious Prince, who loved and understood music'. He treated Bach as a real friend, and was obviously grateful for having him as Capellmeister and director of his chamber music.

The new appointment had one great disadvantage: the religious services at court were not Lutheran. Only 'stern Calvinist psalm-tunes' were to be heard in the royal chapel on Sundays, and Bach's duties did not include playing the organ. He had to neglect 'the betterment of church music' while he was at Cöthen. But he was not altogether cut off from the form of church service he had been brought up on. Prince Leopold's mother was a Lutheran, and before she became a widow she had persuaded her husband to build a Lutheran church in the town. She herself had founded a Lutheran school, so Bach's young children were able to be educated in the way that he wished.

He was now earning more than he had ever earned before. Music meant so much to the Prince that he gave Bach almost the highest salary of anyone at court. And he allowed him and his growing family to live in a wing of the castle. After years in cramped lodgings, Maria Barbara now had lofty rooms with windows looking out on the moat and the tilting-yard, while the children could play in the walled gardens and orchards,

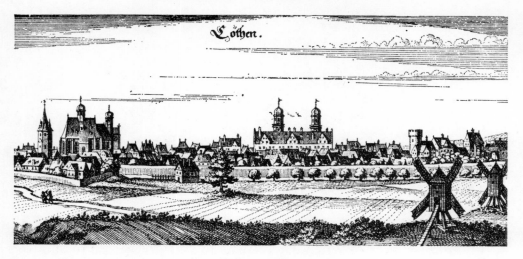

FIG. 9. *Cöthen*

and could marvel at the brightly coloured flowers growing in the ornamental terraces.

Living under the same roof as his patron, Bach had endless opportunities for making music with him. The Prince was not one of those music-
lovers who are content to sit and listen. He played the violin, the viola da
gamba and the harpsichord with his own group of instrumentalists,
whom he had chosen from among the most skilful players in the country.
The long evenings Bach spent in the spacious music room were a welcome
change after the cold severity of Weimar with its 'lights out at 8 p.m.':
at Cöthen the flickering candles must often have burnt down to their
silver sockets while the Prince insisted on repeating the whole of his
Capellmeister's newest concerto. The castle account-books for 1717–23
have been carefully preserved, and we therefore know the names of the
resident soloists who gave the first private performances of Bach's concertos and suites and sonatas. Visiting musicians' names are also mentioned in the lists of expenses, so that when we read of two distinguished
horn-players spending several nights in the castle we can guess that they
were rehearsing the first of the six concertos that Bach dedicated to the
Margrave of Brandenburg.

Whatever instrument he wrote for, Bach always gave his players what

50

FIG. 10. *A viola da gamba player*

Ex.14 RONDEAU

they could enjoy practising. The character of each tune fits the chosen instrument to perfection. Ex. 14 belongs by its very nature to the mellow, light-hearted notes of the flute, while the spiky elegance of Ex. 15 is exactly suited to the more precise articulation of the oboes and bassoon. (If Ex. 15 is tried out on the piano it will be easier with three players, one to each instrumental part.)

Ex.15 TRIO

In his sonatas and suites for unaccompanied violin or cello Bach managed to combine satisfying tunes and skilful technique in a new way that has never been equalled since.

In some of the movements, as in Ex. 16, the music is in two-part counterpoint, to be played on two strings at once.

In other movements, such as the Gigue in Ex. 17, the player keeps to a single melodic line. But the listener never feels the need for any additional accompaniment, because the notes of the tune have grown out of the silently-heard chords that Bach had in his mind when he was writing the music. And these silently-heard chords can make themselves felt, as soon as one gets to know the tune really well. (The tune in Ex. 17 is so completely satisfying that it is even able to carry on an imaginary conversation with itself: the brief comments marked *piano* might almost be part of a dialogue.)

53

Ex.16 ANDANTE

Ex.17 GIGUE

Instrumental Music at Cöthen

We cannot be sure that Prince Leopold was a good enough player to perform the unaccompanied suites, but we can be fairly certain that he practised the three sonatas for viola da gamba and harpsichord with the help of the composer. At these times the two men would have forgotten that one was the royal master and the other his paid servant: they would have worked side by side with that close understanding that comes when two friends are rehearsing great music together.

The Prince allowed Bach considerable freedom in his professional life, and he was able to visit other musicians in other towns and cities. On one occasion he went to Halle, hoping to see Handel and to invite him to Cöthen as the Prince's guest. But Handel had left for London that very day, and the two composers never met.

When the Prince went to drink the waters at the fashionable spa at Carlsbad he took Bach with him, with five of his other instrumentalists and one of the precious harpsichords from Cöthen, so that they could make music during the summer evenings. It was in July 1720, at the end of his second visit to Carlsbad, that Bach returned home to find that his wife had died during his absence. For thirteen years she had given him support through all his difficulties, and now she had left him with the four surviving children of the seven who had been born to her: Catharina Dorothea, aged eleven; Wilhelm Friedemann, aged nine, Carl Philipp Emanuel, aged six; and Johann Gottfried Bernhard, aged five.

Bach did what he could for the children, and helped in their education by giving them music lessons. He had already been teaching the eldest boy: his *Little Book of the Keyboard* for Wilhelm Friedemann was begun in January 1720. This 'Clavier-Büchlein,' a paper-bound exercise book with seventy-one closely-written pages, was passed on in turn to the other children. It begins with an explanation of the clefs, including the C clef, which was used a great deal in Bach's time. (See page 43, line 29.) This is followed by a simple five-finger exercise and the 'embellishments' shown in Ex. 8. After that there are keyboard pieces, which become more and more difficult, step by step. Ex. 18 shows how he could write an easy study that is thoroughly enjoyable to play. It is a technical exercise in evenness of touch and time, but it is also a lesson in harmony, for the

Ex.18 PRELUDE

At a moderate speed : evenly flowing

semiquavers can be gathered together to make chords with the left-hand crotchets. There was probably no need for the nine-year-old Friedemann to practise Ex. 18 in solid chords, for he would have been used to recognizing the underlying harmonies in his father's music.

The first volume of *The Forty-eight Preludes and Fugues* was written at Cöthen for the two elder boys. Bach's own title was *The Well-tempered Clavier.* The word 'Clavier' means 'keyboard': it could be used for the harpsichord or the clavichord, and, later on, for the 'fortepiano', which was the ancestor of our modern piano. The adjective 'well-tempered' refers to the system of tuning which was beginning to be used in the early eighteenth century. In those days the octave was not divided into twelve equal semitones as it is today in our 'equal-tempered' keyboard. Composers were not able to modulate into any key they liked, for if the keyboard's G sharps had been tuned to suit the sharp keys they sounded unbearably out of tune when they had to be used as A flats. Bach always encouraged tuners to 'temper' their semitones more evenly, and he had such faith in the new system of tuning that he wrote a prelude and fugue in every major and minor key, as exercises for his children.

It was while he was still composing pieces for Friedemann's *Clavier-Büchlein* that he found the right step-mother for his children in Anna Magdalena Wilcken, the twenty-year-old daughter of a court trumpeter from Thuringia. She was a professional soprano who had been engaged to sing at Cöthen during the autumn of 1720: they were married in the castle in December 1721. In the 'Note-book' he wrote for her as a present he included some of his loveliest songs: the tune in Ex. 19 sings of the quiet

Ex.19   From Anna Magdalena's Note-book

Fairly slow: always smooth and expressive

content and security that can only be found when accepting God's will.

It seemed as though the settled, happy life in Cöthen might continue. But it was interrupted. For the Prince also got married, and his wife disliked music. She couldn't understand why her husband wanted to practise every day, and she was jealous of the long hours he spent in playing sonatas with his Capellmeister. Bach had hoped that he might work for the Prince for the rest of his life, but after a few months it was obvious that he would have to find a new employer.

The decision to move was made easier for him when he realised that in all his six years at Cöthen he had written no music for the church. At the beginning of 1723 the post of Cantor at St. Thomas's Church in Leipzig became vacant, and he made up his mind to apply for it.

VII

Director of Music in Leipzig

From the very beginning the Leipzig authorities treated Bach ungraciously. They had hoped to persuade the celebrated composer Telemann to accept the post of Cantor and Director of Music at St. Thomas's Church and Choir School, but Telemann preferred writing theatre music in Hamburg to teaching boys in a school in Leipzig. The disappointed members of the City Council therefore had to consider the claims of other possible candidates, including Bach. A paragraph in the minutes of their meeting in April 1723 sums up their deliberations by stating: 'Since we cannot get the best man, we must put up with a mediocre one.'

Only a fortnight before this committee meeting they had heard Bach conduct the first performance of his *St. John Passion* at the Good Friday service in St. Thomas's Church. He had probably been hoping for an occasion to set the story of the Passion to music ever since his visit to Lübeck, nearly twenty years before this, when he had listened to Buxtehude's dramatic contrasts between Good and Evil. In the *St. John Passion* the drama is overwhelming: the angry crowds mutter or shout with a cruel edge to their voices, and the Narrator declaims his story with a poignancy that is unforgettable. The Leipzig congregation had never dreamed that such music could be performed in a church: an old lady sitting in the front pew was heard to say 'Good gracious! One might just as well be at the opera!'

Complaints may have reached the members of the City Council,

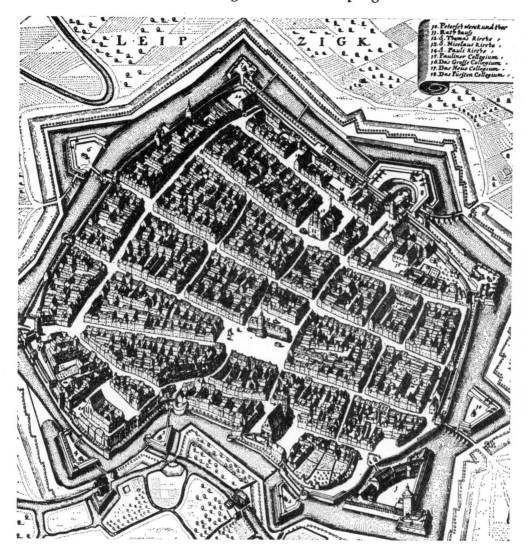

FIG. 11. *Plan of Leipzig, with St. Thomas's Church in the centre foreground*

for at their next committee meeting they decided that if Bach were appointed he should be told that his music must not be 'theatrical'. Soon afterwards, Bach signed the official document and pledged himself to undertake all that was required of him.

61

His duties included playing the organ on alternate Sundays at St. Thomas's Church and St. Nicholas's Church, providing fifty-nine cantatas a year, and rehearsing his pupils in the music to be sung and played during the Sunday services. For one week out of every four the Cantor had to act as Inspector in the school; taking morning and evening prayers; seeing that the boys were called at 5 a.m. in summer and 6 a.m. in winter; calling the register when they had assembled in the practice room on the second floor; saying grace before meals and supervising the reading of a portion of Bible history while the meals were being eaten. After evening prayers he had to be sure that no one was missing and that no lights were taken into the dormitories.

Working conditions in the school were unnecessarily difficult, for there was little organised planning. Every day-to-day request for books and writing material had to go through several stages of a committee meeting. Bach's predecessor had had to address a petition to the Council for 'a board with nails in it to be fixed in the church so that the violins could be hung on it', and he had had to beg for some violin-cases to protect the instruments while they were carried from one church to the other during bad weather. And every petition had to begin with the words: 'Honoured and most Noble, Steadfast; Honoured and most Learned; also Honoured and most Wise Sirs; Honoured and most Gracious Patrons!'

Discipline in the school was precariously maintained by the threat of heavy fines. There were fines for losing the key of the door, for swearing, for not getting up in the morning, for missing prayers, for not tidying the cubicles and for scribbling on the walls with charcoal. A large notice warned the boys: 'Food may *not* be taken into church!' This rule must have been particularly hard to keep, for the long Sunday service went on from 7 a.m. until mid-day. And the boys had no chance of letting their minds wander during the sermon, for they had to write down what they could remember of it after the service was over. In the winter, as a special concession, the younger children were allowed to go back to their schoolroom during the sermon 'if the cold was beyond their endurance'.

Bach's lodgings were in the over-crowded school building. After the spacious freedom of the castle and park at Cöthen it must have taken

FIG. 12. *St. Thomas's Church and School in 1723*

some time to get used to the small rooms and the noisy city streets. His own composing-room was separated by a thin lath-and-plaster partition from one of the junior class-rooms. Here he set to work 'for the betterment

63

of church music', writing for his first Christmas in Leipzig a triumphant setting of the *Magnificat* that is brimful of splendour and happiness.

His work as a school-teacher was more of a burden than a delight. He once admitted to a friend that he found it 'not very agreeable to become a Cantor after having been a Capellmeister'. He would have put up with this, however, if his employers had treated him reasonably. A lot of his time had to be wasted in legal arguments. The University authorities refused to pay all that they owed him for playing the organ at various academic ceremonies. In the end he had to appeal to his 'most Gracious Sovereign', saying that he had only been paid half his lawful stipend. As in all things, he was meticulous about the details of the case, and before sending in his petition to the king he took the trouble to obtain written statements from the widows of his predecessors, stating exactly how much money their husbands had received for playing on similar occasions.

There were endless petty intrigues and jealousies. The organist of the University Church of St. Paul's resented the fact that Bach had been commissioned to write a Funeral Ode for the late Queen: he wanted Bach to sign a statement that he would never again agree to compose any music for St. Paul's. Bach refused, and the harassed University Clerk who had taken the document round to his lodgings had to return with it unsigned. 'I did what I could with him, from 11 till 12,' he reported, 'but without success'.

Then there was a quarrel over the choice of hymns at St. Thomas's. The Cantor had always had the right to choose them, but the Sub-deacon objected to Bach's choice. The usual committee meeting had to be summoned to discuss the matter, and the Superintendent was instructed to inform the Cantor that he must accept the list of hymns that had been drawn up for him. 'But some of them have as many as thirty verses!' Bach protested. The arguments continued, and precious time was wasted that should have been spent on rehearsing or composing.

Another quarrel was about the auditions for new singers in the choir. In 1729 there were several vacancies to be filled, so Bach heard twenty-three candidates and wrote a detailed report of their musical qualifications. The Council ignored his report and admitted four singers he had described as 'useless' and one he had not even heard.

It was in this same year of 1729 that the congregation of St. Thomas's Church listened to the first performance of Bach's *St. Matthew Passion,* one of the greatest masterpieces the world has ever known. The music made no impression whatsoever on the authorities who employed him. They had not reckoned on having a genius to work for them, and they would have been far happier with an orthodox school-teacher.

Eighteen months later they voiced their growing dissatisfaction at a council meeting. 'The Cantor does nothing,' they complained. They were thinking of his visits to other towns to try out new organs or to give recitals. And they were thinking of the way he left a good deal of the routine teaching to deputies. It never occurred to them that no deputy on earth could have written the *St. Matthew Passion.* They considered his behaviour 'incorrigible', and decided, by seven votes to four, to reduce his salary.

Bach replied by sending them a carefully written report in which he mentioned what he considered the minimum requirements for a school of music such as St. Thomas's. He pointed out that some of the students were put into the choir before they could sing in time or in tune. He told them that the instrumentalists were expected to sight-read whatever was put in front of them, because there was no money to pay for adequate rehearsals. 'Our players', he wrote, 'are in a position where they just have to do the best they can. The necessity for earning their living allows them hardly any time for improving their technique.'

The Leipzig authorities took no notice of Bach's 'short and much-needed statement of the requirements of church music', and he began to think about leaving. He wrote to his old school-friend Erdmann, who had been with him at Ohrdruf and Lüneburg, saying: ' . . . It is now nearly four years since you were good enough to answer the last letter I wrote to you, when you asked for news of me . . . It has pleased God that I should be called to Leipzig as Director of Music and Cantor of St. Thomas's School, . . . and here I have remained until now. But I have discovered that (1) the position I hold is not as good as it was represented to be, (2) various fees in connection with the work are no longer paid, (3) the place is very expensive to live in, and (4) my employers are very odd sort of people who don't seem to care much about music. As a result, I have to put up with continual annoyance and persecution. I have therefore decided, with God's help, to try to find employment elsewhere. If you should hear of a suitable appointment in your city, I beg you to recommend me. . . .'

But his friend had no suggestions to make, and Bach stayed on at Leipzig for the remaining twenty years of his life.

VIII

Composing and Teaching

If Bach had really wanted to leave Leipzig he would have gone on searching for another post until he had found one. There were new churches being built in many towns in Germany, and in some of the city churches old organists were retiring. It is difficult to believe that he would not have been welcomed wherever he had wanted to go, yet several years before this he had applied for the post of organist in an important church in Hamburg and had found to his dismay that the successful candidate was supposed to pay a large sum of money for the honour of being accepted. He withdrew his name from the list of applicants, and the committee appointed a man who had been dismissed by the examiners as incompetent but who had offered to pay 4000 marks (£10). (The Pastor of the church, who had been looking forward to having Bach with him, felt it was such an outrage that he preached a Christmas sermon saying that if one of the angels who had sung to the shepherds on the first Christmas Eve had come down from heaven and applied for the post of organist in Hamburg he would have been turned away unless he had brought a sufficiently large offering with him.)

It was in October 1730 that Bach told his friend Erdmann that he wanted to leave Leipzig. A few weeks later he changed his mind. A new Rector was appointed to St. Thomas's; a warm-hearted, enthusiastic teacher called Gesner, who had known Bach in the Weimar years. Everyone liked him. He persuaded the City Council to behave more reasonably.

He improved the living conditions at the school, building larger and more comfortable class-rooms and dormitories. He took a genuine interest in the every-day life of his pupils, discussing with them what they wanted to do when they grew up. He even found time to listen to their choir practices. For he shared Bach's belief that the aim of music was 'the glory of God', and when his school-boys had to go out on a winter's morning to sing at a funeral in one of the city churches he encouraged them by telling them that their duties were a privilege linking them to the angelic choirs of heaven.

Gesner had always admired Bach's music, and now that they were working together he was able to enjoy hearing each new cantata performed. He once described Bach taking a rehearsal, saying: 'he has rhythm in every limb of his body, and all the harmonies are gathered up in his sensitive ear. He keeps everything going, brisking up the backward, and giving confidence to the timid'.

Another eye-witness account of Bach taking a rehearsal mentions that he was remarkably definite and insistent about keeping the tempo, 'which he generally took very lively'. But the writer goes on to say that 'it was seldom he had the good fortune to find a worthy group of performers'. If a distinguished flautist or bassoon player happened to be visiting Leipzig that week he would write a special obbligato tune for them to play in the new cantata. On other Sundays he had to depend on local amateurs for any extra instruments he needed.

His own minimum requirements for his cantatas were '2 (or even 3) first violins, 2 second violins, 2 first violas, 2 second violas, 2 cellos, 1 violone, 2 flutes, 2 or if necessary 3 oboes, 1 or 2 bassoons, 3 trumpets and timpani'. In Leipzig, however, he had only eight professional players: four wind, three strings, and one 'assistant'. And the normal number of singers in his choir was five sopranos, two altos, three tenors and seven basses. It is difficult to imagine how he could have performed his cantatas with such an inadequate choir and orchestra. But, as one of his pupils has told us, he believed that 'everything must be possible'.

This golden rule was perhaps in his mind when he began writing his *B Minor Mass*, a large-scale work needing superb singers and players.

FIG. 13. *A bassoon player*

FIG. 14. *A flautist*

Composing and Teaching

It may seem strange that he should have wanted to set the words of the Mass to music, but in the Lutheran church the *Kyrie* and the *Gloria* were sung in Greek and Latin as a normal part of the service. It was these two movements that he was planning to send to the new King, Augustus III, who was a Roman Catholic. He hoped the king would show his royal gratitude by making him Court Composer. This was a part-time post which Bach would have been able to combine with his work at Leipzig. It would have given him more opportunities for writing instrumental music; and having it would have meant that he had more authority in any arguments with the City Council. It would also have given him more money to live on. In those days there was no Performing Right Society, and composers earned nothing by the music they wrote. Royal patrons gave presents, but the Leipzig councillors considered that Bach's cantatas for St. Thomas's had already been paid for out of his annual salary as Director of Music. Now that he had a second growing family of young children he needed all the additional fees he could earn. Weddings and funerals were the only 'extras' to be relied on, but in one of his letters he mentions that Leipzig was 'unfortunately such a healthy place' that his fees for funerals had gone down by about 100 kroner (£9 10s.) a year.

The *Kyrie* and *Gloria* were finished by the late summer of 1733, and he sent them to the king with a letter of dedication saying: 'With deepest devotion I offer your Majesty this small work as an example of my knowledge of music, begging that your Majesty will be pleased to admit me to your Court.' But Augustus III could think of nothing but the political situation in Poland, and the gift was never acknowledged. Bach persevered in his efforts. By the autumn of 1734 Augustus had been proclaimed king at Cracow, and when he passed through Leipzig on a ceremonial visit Bach seized the opportunity to greet him with a special cantata, performed by his pupils with trumpets and drums. It was an evening performance in the market place, and six hundred students from the University stood in the square, holding lighted torches. The entertainment cost 299 thalers (£74 15s.), most of which was spent on the illuminations. The following day, which happened to be the King's

Ex.20 'Sleepers wake!'
Not too slow

etc.

birthday, Bach performed yet another royal cantata, but his request for the post of Court Composer remained unanswered and he had to wait more than a year before he achieved what he wanted.

By that time he had finished the other movements of his stupendous *B Minor Mass*. Among all his works, this is the one that gives us the clearest picture of his musical personality. As always in his music, the shape of each tune is guided by the meaning of the words. At 'came down from heaven', the violins' quavers drift calmly downwards from the highest to the lowest string: at 'ascended into heaven' the bass singers rise in an effortless arpeggio from their lowest to their highest notes. In the prolonged hush before the expected 'resurrection of the dead' the harmonies move through remote regions that had never before been explored. And in the final 'grant us Thy peace', the piercing notes of the trumpets mount higher and higher to their climax of gratitude.

It is not only in his great masterpieces that Bach conveys such character in his music: it can be heard in each of the Sunday cantatas, whether it is the warm courage of determination in the Advent tune in Ex. 20 or the frosty stillness of the Christmas shepherds' music in Ex. 21.

Composing must have been easier for him during the four years when Gesner was in charge of St. Thomas's. But at the end of 1734 a new Rector, called Ernesti, was appointed, and the easy, companionable way of life was over. Ernesti was a young man of twenty-seven whose aim was 'progressive secularization.' He considered music in school a waste of time. When he found one of Bach's keenest pupils practising the violin during a free period he sneered at him, saying: 'Hm! So you mean to be a beer-house fiddler when you grow up, I suppose.'

Ernesti insisted that he had the right to appoint the prefects who were to take choir practices whenever Bach was on duty at the other churches. One of the boys he chose was so incompetent that he couldn't even beat time in a straightforward hymn tune without turning four-four into three-four and three-four into four-four.

As soon as Bach saw what was happening he turned the boy out of the choir gallery and asked a more musical prefect to conduct the hymns. Ernesti retaliated by forbidding the choir to sing under anyone Bach

73

appointed. This led to 'a disorderly scuffle at Vespers'. One can imagine Bach's agitated state of mind when, as Inspector for the week, he had to take his place with the whole school at supper that evening. He wrote to the Council, saying: 'The Rector has seriously weakened, if indeed he has not wholly undermined, my authority over the pupils.' The Council did nothing about it, and this particular quarrel was kept up for more than two years before it wore itself out. And during those two years Bach could never avoid meeting Ernesti, for unfortunately their rooms were next door to each other.

Meanwhile there were other nagging worries. A critic called Scheibe, an 'inordinately self-esteemed man', wrote an ill-natured article on Bach's music, saying that his works were 'turgid and sophisticated instead of simple and natural'. It is seldom that a good composer is upset by anything a critic says about him; after all, the critic cannot hope to be his equal in understanding, or he would be composing the music himself instead of just writing his opinions about it. But Bach cared above all things for simplicity and naturalness in music, and when Scheibe mistook his skilful technique for artificiality it must have seemed as if he were accusing him of being insincere. Instead of allowing this ill-mannered attack to be forgotten, Bach's friends rushed into print in his defence, and the altercation went on and on, like those embittered 'Letters to the Editor' that go to and fro in the newspapers.

Life became easier during the winter of 1736, for he was at long last appointed Court Composer to Augustus III, and the royal protection helped him in his quarrels with the Council. He was able to get on with his own work, and could enjoy teaching those of his pupils who were really musical. Several of them have left a written account of what they could remember about his lessons in composition: 'From the very beginning he looked for the invention of musical ideas, and advised anyone who was lacking in them to keep off composition altogether.' 'In his criticism of a student's work he could be very severe if the harmony was weak. But he encouraged everything that was really promising, and would give his blessing to a beginner's efforts, even if they showed signs of human weakness.' 'In his lessons he did not waste time over deep

Ex. 21 From the Christmas Oratorio

FIG. 15. *A performance of church music in the early eighteenth century*

theoretical speculations, but began straight away with things that were practical, omitting all the *dry species* of counterpoint.'

We are also told that 'in his harmony exercises he at first set the basses himself and made his pupils invent only the alto and tenor to them. By degrees, he let them also make the basses. He considered his parts as if they were persons who conversed together like a select company. If there were three, each could sometimes be silent and listen to the others till it again had something to the purpose to say. But if in the midst of the most interesting part of the discourse some importunate strange notes suddenly rushed in and attempted to say a word, or even a syllable, without sense, Bach looked on this as a great irregularity that was never to be permitted. With all his strictness he allowed his pupils great liberties. In the use of the intervals, in the turns of the melody and harmony, he let them dare whatever they would and could, [for] he took it for granted that all his pupils in composition were able to think musically.'

One of the best descriptions of his keyboard lessons is given in a biographical note written by the son of one of his Leipzig pupils: 'The great Sebast. Bach accepted my father as a pupil and greeted him with particular kindness because he came from his own part of the country. At the first lesson he set his Inventions before him. When he had studied these to Bach's satisfaction, there followed a series of Suites; then *The Well-tempered Clavier*. This latter work Bach played altogether *three times through* for him, and my father counted these among his happiest hours.'

There must have been many harpsichord pupils who were grateful to their teacher for having written those preludes and fugues for his own children to practise.

The three elder sons had left home by the time he was appointed Court Composer. They were now working as professional musicians: Wilhelm Friedemann in Dresden, Carl Philipp Emanuel in Frankfurt, and Johann Gottfried Bernhard in Mühlhausen. Bach missed their help, particularly in copying out the instrumental parts for the cantatas. Anna Magdalena managed to do a tremendous amount of copying for him, in spite of her large family of small children. She became such a good copyist that it is often difficult to tell at a first glance whether a manuscript is in her writing or in Bach's.

Very few of his works were published during his life, and it must have been a continual struggle to get the parts written out in time for the weekly rehearsals. Someone once calculated that it would take an ordinary music copyist sixty years to copy out all the scores Bach wrote. It seems unbelievable, when we remember that he was a performer and a teacher, as well as a composer. But geniuses are endowed with an extra supply of energy to help them to get through the day's work and to enable them to live the sort of life in which 'everything must be possible.'

PLATE III. *Bach's musical handwriting*

PLATE IV. *Bach in the last year of his life*

IX

The Last Twelve Years

In 1738 one of Bach's many cousins came to live with him. This was Johann Elias, the grandson of Bach's father's elder brother. He was studying divinity at Leipzig University, and he repaid Bach's hospitality by becoming tutor to the three younger boys: Gottfried Heinrich, aged fourteen; Johann Christoph Friedrich, aged six, and Johann Christian, aged three.

Elias was a kindly, competent young man, and Bach found it a great help having him in the house. 'My cousin assures me that he will need me to stay here for some time to come,' Elias told his own family. 'It seems there is no one who can take over my duties if I am away.' In another letter home he asked for some yellow carnation plants to be sent to Anna Magdalena for her garden: when they arrived they 'gave her more pleasure than children find in their Christmas gifts', and 'she nurtured them tenderly, lest harm should befall them'. Elias also tried to buy her a tame linnet which Bach had heard singing 'like an accomplished artist'. And he arranged for a cask of sweet muscat wine to be sent by carrier, 'to give his cousin pleasure, in return for the many benefits he had received in his house'. A second present of wine, sent in Elias's absence, came to grief on the way, and Bach wrote to him, saying: 'Unfortunately the cask was damaged during the journey, for it arrived one-third empty. It is a pity that even the smallest drop of such a noble a gift of God should be wasted, but I am none the less heartily obliged by my cousin's present.'

79

During the four years that he was with them, Elias acted as Bach's secretary, keeping a watchful eye on the manuscript scores. There is a letter in which he refuses his own brother-in-law the loan of a cantata: 'My cousin regrets he cannot send it; he has lent the parts to a singer who has not returned them. He won't allow the score out of his hands, for he has lost several works by lending them to other people.'

Elias's help was particularly welcome at this time, for Bach was in great distress about his third son, Gottfried Bernhard. The young man had been organist at a church in Mühlhausen, but had got into debt and had had to leave. Bach settled all the claims for money and recommended him for an organist's post in Sangerhausen. But after working there for a few months, Bernhard neglected his duties at the church and became even more deeply involved in debt. Bach knew nothing of this further disgrace until the arrival of a letter from a friend in Sangerhausen, telling him that Bernhard had walked out of his lodgings without leaving any address. It was the worst grief that Bach had yet known. 'My loving care has failed to help him', he wrote. 'I must bear my cross in patience, leaving my undutiful son to God's unfailing mercy.' Bernhard never came home again. Without telling his father, he began studying law at Jena University, only a few miles from Leipzig. He may have intended to come home during the summer vacation, but before he had finished his first year as a student he became seriously ill with fever, and died.

The two other sons of his first marriage were a source of joy and pride. Friedemann was sometimes able to come over from Dresden and take part in the family music-making: we are told that on these occasions Bach preferred to play viola, as it was 'in the middle of the harmony'. Friedemann once brought two celebrated lute-players with him, and Elias wrote to a friend saying they had had 'something extra fine in the way of chamber music in the Cantor's rooms'.

Musicians who were passing through Leipzig always called in at the house, and however busy Bach was, he found time to welcome them. Several of them spoke afterwards of his 'excellent amiability and unfeigned love of his neighbours'. His own children have described their home as 'like a beehive, and just as full of life'.

Ex.22 'From heav'n on high I come to earth'

At a moderate speed

etc.

The Last Twelve Years

The local musicians in Leipzig were becoming more friendly, now that most of the quarrels and jealousies were over. In the summer of 1747 they elected him a member of the Society for the Promotion of Musical Science, and for his 'diploma' he wrote them a set of canonic variations on the well-known Christmas carol, 'From heav'n on high I come to earth'. (See Ex. 22. It can be played by two violins and a cello; or by three pianists at one keyboard if the top line is played an octave higher.)

This set of variations is a wonderful example of Bach's skill in turning a tune upside down or back to front without letting the cleverness interfere with the enjoyment of the music. He was able to think in canon, just as a mathematician can think in equations and a classical scholar can think in Latin. As soon as he heard a tune, he began turning it into counterpoint in his mind. Carl Philipp Emanuel has described how his father used to listen to an organist improvising a fugue: 'he could soon say, after the first entry of the tune, what devices it would be possible to use; and whenever I happened to be standing near him he would whisper to me what he expected to hear, and would joyfully nudge me as soon as his guesses were proved right.'

It was in this same year of 1747 that Bach visited Carl Philipp Emanuel in Berlin, to get to know his daughter-in-law and to see his first grandchild. Emanuel was now accompanist to Frederick the Great, who was an enthusiastic flute player. Bach hoped to hear the royal orchestra at Potsdam, for there was a concert in the palace every evening, with the king playing first flute and choosing the programme himself and 'even placing the parts on the orchestral stands.' On the evening of Bach's visit the concert was just going to begin when one of the attendants told the king that Bach had arrived at the palace. Frederick put down his flute and turned to the members of his orchestra, saying: 'Gentlemen! Old Bach is here!' Having greeted him warmly, the king led him from room to room and invited him to try all his keyboard instruments, including the newly-invented 'fortepiano'. Frederick then played a tune he had made up himself, asking Bach to improvise on it. Bach immediately turned it into a fugue; the king was delighted, and 'all those present were seized with astonishment'.

FIG. 16. *Frederick the Great playing the flute with his orchestra*

The tune was a good one, and when Bach returned to Leipzig he wrote it out and developed it more fully into a work which he called *The Musical Offering*. (See Fig. 17.) He sent the manuscript to the king, saying:

MOST GRACIOUS SOVEREIGN,

With humblest submission I have dedicated to your Majesty a Musical Offering, the most distinguished part of which is the work of your Majesty's own illustrious hand. With profound and agreeable duty I hold in mind your Majesty's gracious condescension when I visited Potsdam, in playing to me on the clavier the theme for a fugue which you commanded me there and then to develop in your royal presence. As in humble

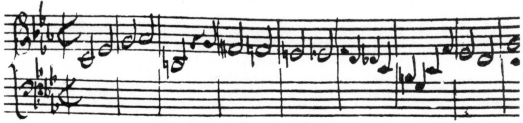

FIG. 17. *The theme of* The Musical Offering, *in Bach's writing*

83

duty bound, I obeyed your Majesty's command. But I was not blind to the fact that, lacking opportunity to study the theme, my performance was not adequate to its excellence. However, I resolved to give a right royal theme the treatment it deserves, and to make it known to the whole world. That resolution I have fulfilled to the best of my ability, with the single and laudable desire to exalt, though in a minor sphere, the fame of a potentate whose greatness, in the realm of music no less than in the arts of war and peace, is acclaimed and admired by all. I am bold to add this humble request—that your Majesty will condescend graciously to accept this little work and continue your favour to

Your Majesty's most obliged and humble servant,

THE AUTHOR

Leipzig, 7 July 1747

The royal theme was still in Bach's mind two years later, for he used a shortened variant of it as the basis of his great instrumental work *The Art of Fugue*, where he goes further than any other composer in the miraculous interweaving of tunes in canon.

The Art of Fugue was left unfinished. The manuscript reaches the point where he had just introduced the four letters of his own name in musical notes, B (German for B flat) A, C, H (German for B natural), and then it breaks off. He was too ill to go on any further.

He was so ill during the summer of 1749 that the members of the City Council, with their usual lack of courtesy, began choosing his successor. But he recovered for a time and even found enough energy to fight one more battle against the Rector Ernesti in defence of a gifted pupil.

An operation on his eyes in January 1750 left him very weak and depressed. But there were intervals when his sight improved, and he was able to revise some of his organ works for publication. He was also working on the Eighteen Chorale Preludes, and he had written fifteen of them when he became blind. He asked his son-in-law, who had been a pupil, to come and take down the last three from dictation. The very last chorale was the tune in Ex. 1. This hymn was usually sung to the words 'When we are in the greatest need.' But Bach was hearing the music in his mind's ear as belonging to another set of verses that were sometimes sung to the same tune, and he asked his son-in-law to write the alternative title: 'I come before Thy throne of Grace.'

This was the last music he worked at. A few days later, on July 28th, he died.

X

The Rediscovery of Bach's Music

When Bach was buried, none of the church authorities thought of putting up a tombstone or any other monument in his memory. The City Council met on the day before the funeral to appoint his successor, but no one suggested that a few words of regret or appreciation might be recorded in the minutes of the meeting.

Anna Magdalena had to leave her home. Of the six surviving children out of her family of thirteen, the youngest was eight years old. She wrote a letter to the authorities, applying for the six months' allowance that was always paid to the widows of employees. But the accountant remembered that twenty-seven years ago, when Bach first arrived in Leipzig, he had received full payment for the first quarter although he only began work in February, so the committee subtracted 21 thalers plus 21 groschen (£5 12s.) from the sum that was due to Anna Magdalena. She died ten years later, in an almshouse, and was given a pauper's funeral.

The Art of Fugue was published in 1751, but by 1756 only thirty copies had been sold. After that, it took nearly fifty years for anyone to have the courage to publish a complete work by Bach. In the second half of the eighteenth century, the name 'Bach' meant Carl Philipp Emanuel in Germany and Johann Christian in England. Johann Sebastian's music was considered 'old-fashioned', and was soon forgotten.

The first of the great composers of the late eighteenth century to become excited over the sound of Bach's music was Mozart. He was passing

86

through Leipzig in 1789 when he happened to hear a choir-practice in St. Thomas's. The Cantor who was then in charge of the music had had lessons from Bach forty years before this. (He was the pupil Bach had defended in his final quarrel with the Rector Ernesti.) On this particular occasion he was rehearsing Bach's *Sing to the Lord*. Mozart had heard very little of Bach's music, and the magnificent eight-part motet made an extraordinary impression on him. An onlooker described the scene, saying: 'the choir had hardly begun singing when Mozart sat up, startled; a few bars later he cried out: 'Why, what is this?' And from then onwards his whole soul seemed to be in his ears. When the singing was finished he said, '*Here* is something one can learn from!' He asked to see the other motets, and as there were no scores available he spread the separate parts all round him, 'on his knees, on the floor, and on the chairs that were near him, and, forgetting everything else, did not get up again until he had looked through everything of Bach's that was there.'

This was the beginning of the rediscovery of Bach's music. Beethoven, at the age of twelve, practised *The Well-tempered Clavier*, and years afterwards he organized a benefit concert for Bach's last surviving daughter, who was then an old woman.

Mendelssohn, with great courage, conducted a performance of the *St. Matthew Passion* in Berlin when he was only twenty. It was exactly a hundred years after the first performance in 1729, and the music had not been heard since then.

Mendelssohn's friend Schumann, who taught at the Leipzig Conservatoire, brought up his pupils on Bach fugues. 'Let *The Well-tempered Clavier* be your daily bread,' he told them. 'Then you will become thorough musicians.' He also used to say: 'We are never at an end with Bach. He seems to grow even more wonderful, the oftener he is heard.'

It was Schumann who first suggested bringing out a complete edition of Bach's works. This 'timely and useful undertaking' proved to be a colossal task: the editors of the Bachgesellschaft (or 'Bach Society') soon discovered that many of the manuscripts had been lost. Less than two hundred cantatas had survived, though it is fairly certain that Bach must have written at least two hundred and ninety-five. Other manuscripts were mutilated or incomplete, and it took years and years of patient skill to bring out the volumes that can now be studied in the chief music libraries throughout the world.

The Bachgesellschaft volumes have been printed without editorial additions: the music is just as Bach wrote it. This is a blessing, for nineteenth-century musicians had some very strange ideas about how his music should be performed. They liked to use vast choirs and orchestras, which slowed down the dramatic choruses and made them sound heavy and ponderous. And they liked to interpret the music in the romantic style of their own century, with frequent rallentandos and diminuendos. When we hear an early gramophone record of the first of the *Forty-eight Preludes* being played on the piano with plenty of rubato and sustaining pedal, it sounds 'wrong' to our ears. But we, in our own interpretations, are only guessing what Bach wanted, and our guesses will probably sound 'wrong' before the year 2000.

Each generation has to bring Bach's music to life again in its own way. To a great composer, this is what immortality means. And Bach's music can stand a good deal. It can even stand being used as compulsory test pieces in end-of-term examinations. For, as his earliest biographer has said, 'his tunes never grow old, and his music sounds as fresh today as when it was written'.

A book about Bach should allow his music to have the last word. In the following pages the final chorus from his *St. Matthew Passion* has been arranged so that it can be played on the piano by a solitary reader.

Ex.23 LAST CHORUS from the St. Matthew Passion

D.C.al FINE
(with repeats)

Index

Arnstadt, 15, 28, 33, 35
Augustus III, 71–3, 74

Bach, Anna Magdalena (second wife), 57, 77–8, 79, 86
Bach, Carl Philipp Emanuel (son), 55, 77, 82, 86
Bach, Christoph (cousin), 18
Bach, Johann Ambrosius (father), 16–19
Bach, Johann Christian (son), 79, 86
Bach, Johann Elias (cousin), 79–80
Bach, Johann Christoph (brother), 19–22
Bach, Johann Gottfried Bernhard (son), 55, 77, 80
BACH, JOHANN SEBASTIAN
  Works:
    Art of Fugue, The, 84, 86
    Canon for J. G. Walther, 43
    Canonic Variations,
      'From heav'n on high', 82
    Cantatas:
      Come, Thou Lovely Hour of Dying, 43
      God is My King, 36–7
      Sleepers Wake, 72–3
    Chorale Preludes:
      'A Stronghold Sure', 39

'I come before Thy throne of Grace', 85
Chorale Variations:
  'O God, thou gracious God,' 29
Christmas Oratorio, 73
Forty-eight Preludes and Fugues, The (or *The Well-tempered Clavier*), 22, 57, 77, 87, 88
Little Book of the Keyboard, 55–7
Little Organ Book, 46
Magnificat, 64
Mass in B Minor, 68, 71, 73
Motet:
  Sing to the Lord, 87
Musical Offering, The, 83–4
'Note-book for Anna Magdalena', 57
St. John Passion, 60
St. Matthew Passion, 65, 87
Bach, Maria Barbara (first wife), 34, 35, 49, 55
Bach, Veit (great-great-grandfather), 15–16
Bach, Wilhelm Friedemann (son), 55, 57, 77
Bachgesellschaft, 87–8
Baroque music, 37
Beethoven, Ludwig van, 87
Berlin, 82

Index

Böhm, Georg, 22, 25
Brandenburg, Margrave of, 50
Buxtehude, Dietrich, 22, 32–3, 60
   Evening Music, 32

Canon, 43
Calvinist service, 49
Carlsbad, 55
Cassel, 46
Celle, 25, 27
Chorales:
   'O World, I now must leave thee', 18
   'When we are in the greatest need',
     18
Continuo, 36–7
Cöthen, 48–50, 55, 59, 62

Dornheim, 35
Dresden, 46, 77

Eisenach, 15, 17–19
Erdmann, Georg, 24, 65–6, 67
Ernesti, Johann August, 73–4, 84, 87
Ernst August, Prince, 43, 46

Figured bass, 20–1, 37
Folksongs, 17
Forkel, J. N., 43
Frederick the Great, 82–4
Franck, Salomo, 43
Frankfurt, 77

Gesner, Johann Matthias, 67–8, 73
'Grace-notes', or Ornaments, 27, 55

Halle, 45, 55
Hamburg, 25, 67
Handel, George Frideric, 55
Hymn-tunes, *see* Chorales

Johann Ernst, Prince, 43

Leipzig, 59–87
Leopold, Prince of Anhalt-Cöthen, 46,
   49–50, 55, 59
Löwe, J. J., 25
Lübeck, 32–33, 60
Lüneburg, 22–5, 65
Lutheran church, 15, 17, 18, 49, 71
Luther, Martin, 17, 18

Marchand, Louis, 46
Mendelssohn, Felix, 87
Mozart, Wolfgang Amadeus, 86–7
Mühlhausen, 34, 35–9, 77
Music copying, 24, 77–8

Ohrdruf, 19, 20, 22, 25, 65
Organ-building, 37, 45

Pachelbel, Johann, 22
Palestrina, Giovanni Pierluigi da, 25

Reinken, J. A., 25

Scheibe, Johann Adolph, 74
Schumann, Robert, 87
Schütz, Heinrich, 25

Telemann, Georg Philipp, 60

Vivaldi, Antonio, 43

Walther, Johann Gottfried, 43–5
Weimar, 39–43, 46, 48, 67
Wilhelm Ernst, Duke of Weimar, 40,
   46, 48
Wilcken, Anna Magdalena, *see* Bach,
   Anna Magdalena